Appendix A: Brief Guide to Microsoft Project 2010

from

Revised An Introduction to Project Management, Third Edition

By

Kathy Schwalbe

Professor, Augsburg College

Department of Business Administration

Minneapolis, Minnesota

Appendix A: Brief Guide to Microsoft Project 2010

from

Revised An Introduction to Project Management, Third Edition

Reviewers/Editors

Ray Guidone

Carl Hixon

Cindy Dawson

Brian May

Cover Photo

Dan Schwalbe

Published by Kathy Schwalbe, LLC

Visit **www.kathyschwalbe.com** for more information on this and other books by Kathy Schwalbe.

Note: This text only includes Appendix A, Brief Guide to Microsoft Project 2010. The page numbering is the same as the original text. It was created in April 2010.

Appendix A ....

Brief Guide to Microsoft Project 2010

APPENDIX A:

Project Management Software:

Brief Guide to Microsoft Project 2010

Note: This guide was written using the Beta release of Project 2010 and Windows XP. Your screens may appear slightly different. You can download a free trial of Project 2010 from www.microsoft.com/project. You can access the older version of this guide based on Project 2007 on the companion Web site at www.intropm.com. Students who purchased an older version of this text (*An Introduction to Project Management, Third Edition*, by Kathy Schwalbe) can purchase just this new Appendix from www.intropm.com. Instructors can access the latest guide based on Project 2010 on the instructor site.

INTRODUCTION

There are hundreds of project management software products on the market today. Unfortunately, many people who own the software have no idea how to use it. It is important to understand basic concepts of project management, such as creating a work breakdown structure, determining task dependencies, and so on before making effective use of this software. Many project teams still use spreadsheets or other familiar software to help manage projects. However, if you can master a good project management software tool, it can really help in managing projects. This appendix summarizes basic information on project management software in general. It also provides a brief guide to using Microsoft Office Project 2010 (often referred to as Project 2010), the latest version of the most widely used product. Appendix B provides a brief summary of @task, the most popular totally online tool.

PROJECT MANAGEMENT SOFTWARE REVIEWS

Figure A-1 provides a screen shot showing the top ten project management software products based on a June 2009 review by TopTenREVIEWS™. The products listed in the top ten include:

1. Microsoft Project

2. MindView

3. Project KickStart

4. RationalPlan Multi Project

5. FastTrack Schedule

6. Service Desktop Pro

7. Milestones

8. MinuteMan

9. FusionDesk Professional

10. VIP Team To Do List

Notice that Microsoft Project is number one on the list. Also notice its steep price of over $500 for a single user. Remember that students can purchase Microsoft Project and other software at greatly reduced rates from sites such as www.journeyed.com (only $69.98 for Project 2007 Standard in July 2009). You can also normally download free trials of Project and other software products.

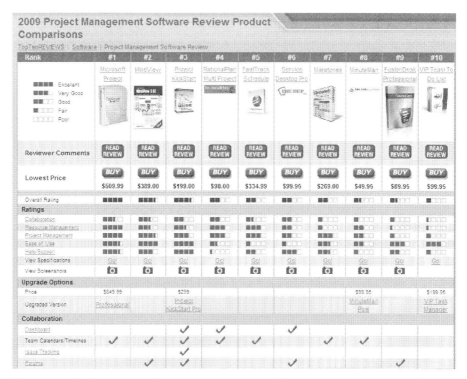

Figure A-1. Top ten project management software product comparisons

Below are descriptions of the criteria for comparing the software products:

- **Collaboration:** How information and issues are communicated with project team members, including email, conference calls, meetings, web-based locations and more. Collaboration should be easy to use.
- **Resource Management: Project management software should** manage and control the resources needed to run a project, such as people, money, time and equipment.
- **Project Management:** The process, practice and activities needed to perform continuous evaluation, prioritization, budgeting and selection of investments are key. Proper project management capabilities provide the greatest value and contribution to the strategic interest of your company.
- **Ease of Use:** All project management software has a learning curve, but the best have functions that are easy to find and simple enough for anyone to use from Day 1, Project 1.
- **Help/Support:** Project management software should offer a comprehensive user guide and help system. The manufacturer should provide email addresses or telephone numbers for direct answers to technical questions.[1]

In addition to reviewing project management software in general, TopTenREVIEWS™ also compared online products in a separate category. These products require an Internet connection for use. Figure A-2 lists the top ten results. The top fourteen products listed include:

1. @task
2. Daptiv PPM
3. Clarizen
4. Project Insight
5. Celoxis
6. Intervals
7. Projecturf
8. Central Desktop
9. Easy Projects NET
10. eStudio
11. Project Office.net
12. Copper
13. Smooth Projects
14. Zoho Projects

@task took the number one spot. Like most tools in this category, @task provides the ability to create Gantt charts, numerous reports and views, project dashboards, and it provides integration with Microsoft Project files. One of its unique features is its support of iPhones. See End Note 1 or visit the Web sites for any of these products and use a free trial version. See Appendix B for more information on using @task.

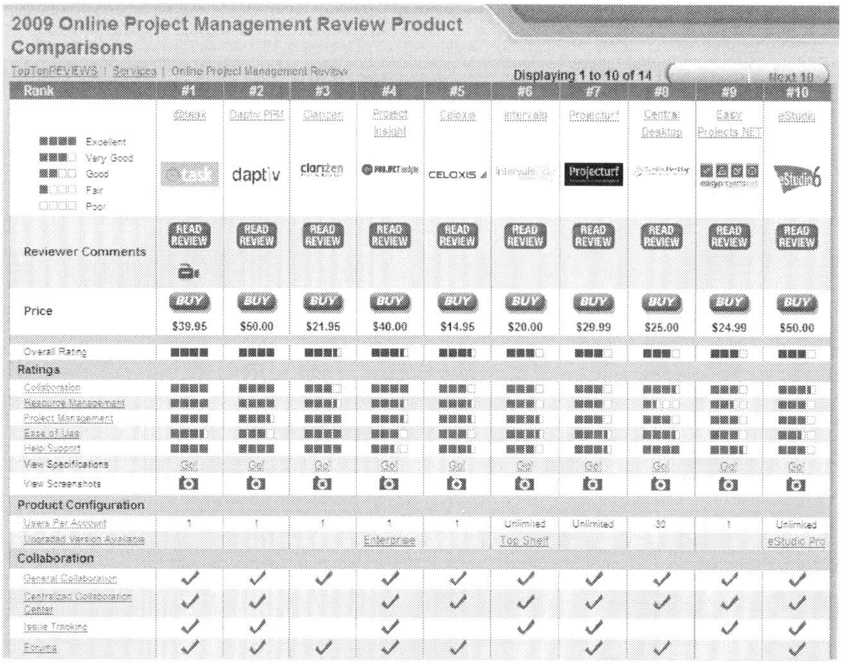

2009 Online Project Management Review Product Comparisons

Figure A-2. Top ten online project management product comparisons

BASIC FEATURES OF PROJECT MANAGEMENT SOFTWARE

What makes project management software different from other software tools? Why not just use a spreadsheet or database to help manage projects?

You can do a lot of project management planning and tracking using non-project management software. You could use a simple word processor to list tasks, resources, dates, and so on. If you put that information into a spreadsheet, you can easily sort it, graph it, and perform other functions. A relational database tool could provide even more manipulation of data. You can use email and other tools to collaborate with others. However, project management software is designed specifically for managing projects, so it normally includes several distinct and important features not found in other software products:

- *Creating work breakdown structures, Gantt charts, and network diagrams*: As mentioned in this text, a fundamental concept of project management is breaking down the scope of the project into a work breakdown structure (WBS). The WBS is the basis for creating the project schedule, normally shown as a Gantt chant. The Gantt chart shows start and end dates of tasks as well as dependencies between tasks, which are more clearly shown in a network diagram. Project management software makes it easy to create a WBS, Gantt chart, and network diagram. These features help the project manager and team visualize the project at various levels of detail.

- *Integrating scope, time, and cost data*: The WBS is a key tool for summarizing the scope of a project, and the Gantt chart summarizes the time or schedule for a project. Project management software allows you to assign cost and other resources to tasks on the WBS, which are tied to the schedule. This allows you to create a cost baseline and use earned value management to track project performance in terms of scope, time, and cost in an integrated fashion.

- *Setting a baseline and tracking progress*: Another important concept of project management is preparing a plan and measuring progress against the plan. Project management software lets you track progress for each task. The tracking Gantt chart is a nice tool for easily seeing the planned and actual schedule, and other views and reports show progress in other areas.

- *Providing other advanced project management features*: Project management software often provides other advanced features, such as setting up different types of scheduling dependencies, determining the critical path and slack for tasks, working with multiple projects, and leveling resources. For example, you can easily set up a task to start when its predecessor is halfway finished. After entering task dependencies, the software should easily show you the critical path and slack for each task. You can also set up multiple projects in a program and perform portfolio management analysis with some products. Many project management software products also allow you to easily adjust resources within their slack allowances to create a smoother resource distribution. These advanced features unique to project management are rarely found in other software tools.

As you can see, there are several important features that are unique to project management software that make them worth using. Next you'll learn what's new in Project 2010 and how to use basic features of Project 2010 Standard.

WHAT'S NEW IN PROJECT 2010

Project 2010 is not just a run-of-the-mill update. Microsoft really listened to users and has revised Project to meet user needs. Learning some of the new features might seem like a chore, but it is well worth the effort.

If you are familiar with Project 2007, it may be helpful to review some of the new features in Project 2010.

- *Improved user interface:* Project 2010 now includes the "ribbon" interface instead of using the old menus and toolbars similar to Office 2003. Commands are organized in logical groups under tabs, such as File, Task, Resource, Project, View, and Format. The File tab takes you to the new Backstage feature, a one-stop graphical destination for opening, saving, and printing your files. You can also now right-click on different items, like a table cell or chart, to bring up commonly used commands quickly.

- *New viewing options:* Project 2010 includes several new views. A timeline view is automatically displayed above other views to show you a concise overview of the entire project schedule. You can easily add tasks to the timeline, print it, or paste it into an e-mail. The new team planner view lets you quickly see what your team members are working on, and you can move tasks from one person to another using this view. For example, if a resource is overallocated, you can drag a task to another resource to remove the overallocation. You can also add new columns quickly and use the new zoom slider at the lower right of the screen to zoom your schedule in and out. Also, the tab for viewing and printing reports is easier to navigate with more options for visual reports.

- *Manual scheduling:* Unlike previous versions of Project where tasks were automatically scheduled, Project 2010 uses manual schedule as its default. In past versions of Project, summary tasks were automatically calculated based on their subtasks. Resources were also adjusted automatically. With Project 2010, this is no longer the case. For example, you might want to enter durations for summary tasks and then fill in the detailed information for their subtasks later. When you open a new file, Project reminds you that new tasks are manually scheduled and lets you easily switch to automatic scheduling, if desired. You can also use the new compare versions to see Gantt bars to more clearly see how one version of a project differs from another version.

- *Improved collaboration:* Project 2010 is able to provide an interface with the most popular portals used in industry. Project now uses SharePoint instead of Project Web Access for collaboration. Project Server 2010 also provides integration with Microsoft Exchange 2010 to enable team members to manage and report on tasks directly from Microsoft Outlook. Remember that Project Standard does not include these collaboration features. You must have Project Professional and Project Server to use the enterprise features of Project.

Next, you will learn some basic information about Project 2010 and explore the main screen elements and Help facility.

USING PROJECT 2010

Before you can use Project 2010 or any project management software effectively, you must understand the fundamental concepts of project management, such as creating work breakdown structures (WBS), linking tasks, entering duration estimates, assigning resources, and so on. Make sure you read most of this text before using Project 2010 so you understand these concepts. This text provides instructions for using the stand-alone version of Project 2010 known as Project Standard. Project Professional and the Enterprise version of Project require special server software to perform online and collaborative functions. Consult Microsoft's Web site for detailed information on other products.

Before You Begin

This appendix assumes you are using Project 2010 with Windows XP, Vista, or Windows 7 and are familiar with other Windows-based applications. Check your work by reviewing the many screen shots included in the steps, or by using the solution files that are available for download from the companion Web site for this text or from your instructor.

> **NOTE**: *You need to be running Windows XP, Vista, or Windows 7 to use Project 2010.* It does not run on Macintosh computers or other operating systems. Most organizations have Project 2010 as part of their license if they have Office 2010. You can download a free trial from www.microsoft.com/project. Students can purchase a full version of Project Standard from sites like www.journeyed.com for around $69.

This appendix uses a fictitious project—Project A+—to illustrate how to use the software. The WBS for Project A+ uses the five project management process groups as level 2 items (initiating, planning, executing, monitoring and controlling, and closing). Standard deliverables under each of those process groups are included, as described in this text. Each section of the appendix includes hands-on activities for you to perform.

> **NOTE:** To complete the hands-on activities in the appendix, you will need to download files from the companion Web site for this text (*www.intropm.com*) to your computer. When you begin each set of steps, make sure you are using the correct file. Before you begin your work you should have Customer Feedback.mpp file. Save the files you create yourself in a different folder so you do not write over the ones you download.

In addition, you will create the following files from scratch as you work through the steps:

- wbs.mpp
- schedule.mpp

You will also use the following file to create a hyperlink:

- stakeholder_register.doc

Next you will learn how to start Project 2010, review the Help facility and a template file, and begin to plan Project A+.

Overview of Project 2010

The first step to mastering Project 2010 is to become familiar with the major screen elements and the Help facility. This section describes each of these features.

Starting Project 2010 and Understanding the Main Screen Elements

To start Project 2010:

1. *Open Project 2010.* Click the **Start** button on the taskbar, point to **All Programs** in Windows XP or **Programs** in Vista or Windows 7, point to **Microsoft Office**, and then click **Microsoft Office Project 2010**. Alternatively, a shortcut or icon might be available on the desktop; in this case, double-click the icon to start the software.

2. *Maximize Project 2010.* If the Project 2010 window does not fill the entire screen as shown in Figure A-3, click the **Maximize** button in the upper-right corner of the window.

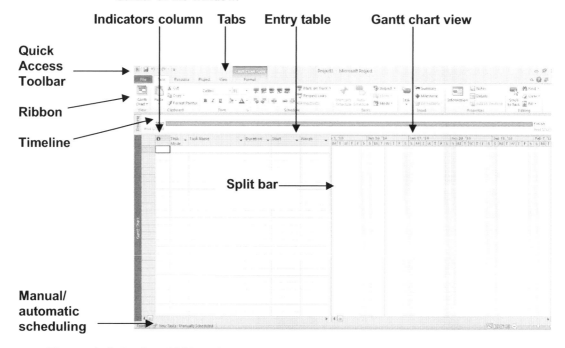

Figure A-3. Project 2010 main screen

Project 2010 is now running and ready to use. Look at some of the elements of the screen.

- The Ribbon, tabs, and Quick Access toolbar are similar to other Office 2007 or 2010 applications.

- The timeline view is displayed below the ribbon.

- The default manual scheduling for new tasks is on the lower left of the screen. You can click that option to switch to automatic scheduling.

- The default view is the Gantt chart view, which shows tasks and other information as well as a calendar display. You can access other views by clicking the View command button on the far left side of the ribbon.

- The areas where you enter information in a spreadsheet-like table are part of the Entry table. For example, you can see entry areas for Task Name, Duration, Start, and Finish.

- You can make the Entry table more or less wide by using the Split bar. When you move the mouse over the split bar, your cursor changes to the resize pointer. Clicking and dragging the split bar to the right reveals other task information in the Entry table, including Predecessors, Resource Names, and Add New columns.

- The column to the left of the Task Name column in the Entry table is the Indicators column. The Indicators column displays indicators or symbols related to items associated with each task, such as task notes or hyperlinks to other files.

Notice that when Project 2010 starts, it opens a new file named Project1, as shown in the title bar. If you open a second file, the name will be Project2, and so on, until you save and rename the file.

Using Project Help and the Project Web Site

You can access information to help you learn how to use Project 2010. Figure A-4 shows the detailed list of topics available from Project Help. You can access help by Pressing F1 or clicking on the question mark/help icon on upper right side of the ribbon. Remember this feature requires an Internet connection.

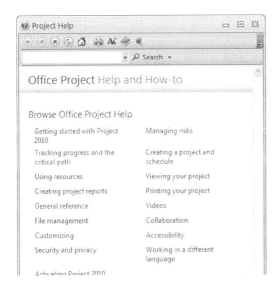

Figure A-4. Topics under Project help

Microsoft provides a number of resources on its Web site to help you learn how to use Project 2010. They provide product information, help and how-to guides on various versions of Project, training information, and templates. Microsoft's Web site for Project 2010 (*www.microsoft.com/project*) provides files for users to download, case studies, articles, and other useful materials. Figure A-5 shows a screen shot of this Web site from March 2010. See the companion Web site for this text for updated information on Project and other resources.

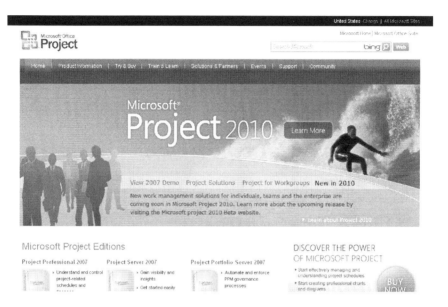

Figure A-5. Microsoft Office Project web site (www.microsoft.com/project)

Many features in Project 2010 are similar to ones in other Windows programs. For example, to collapse or expand tasks, click the appropriate symbols to the left of the task name. To access shortcut items, right-click in either the Entry table area or the Gantt chart. Many of the Entry table operations in Project 2010 are very similar to operations in Excel. For example, to adjust a column width, click and drag or double-click between the column heading titles.

Next, you will get some hands-on experience by opening an existing file to explore various screen elements. Project 2010 comes with several template files, and you can also access templates from Microsoft Office Online or other Web sites.

EXPLORING PROJECT 2010 USING AN EXISTING FILE

To open a file and adjust Project 2010 screen elements:

1. *Open an existing file.* Click the **File tab**, then select **Open**, and browse to find the file named **Customer Feedback.mpp** that you copied from the

companion Web site for this text (www.intropm.com), and then **double-click** the filename to open the file. (This file is a template file that comes with Project 2007 where it is called Customer Feedback Monitoring.) Your screen should resemble Figure A-6.

Task Note Need to widen column   Split Bar

Indicator

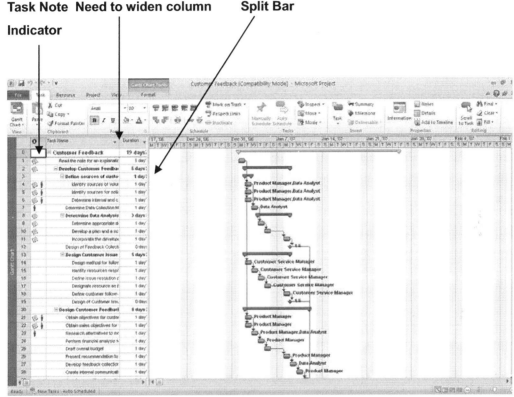

Figure A-6. Customer Feedback.mpp file

2. Widen the Task Name column. Move the **cursor** between the Task Name and Duration column, then **double-click** to widen the Task Name column so all of the text shows.

3. Move the Split Bar. Move the **Split Bar** to the right so only the entire Task Name column is visible.

4. View the first Note. Move your mouse over the yellow **Notes symbol** in the Indicators column for Task 2and read its contents. It is a good idea to provide a short note describing the purpose of project files.

5. Add the Timeline and a task to it. Check the **Timeline** box under the View tab, Split View group. If you cannot see the entire project schedule, as shown in Figure A-7, click the **Zoom** button or **Zoom slider** to make adjustments. Click on the Task Name for **Task 12**, click the **Task** tab, and then click the **Add to Timeline** button under the Properties group.

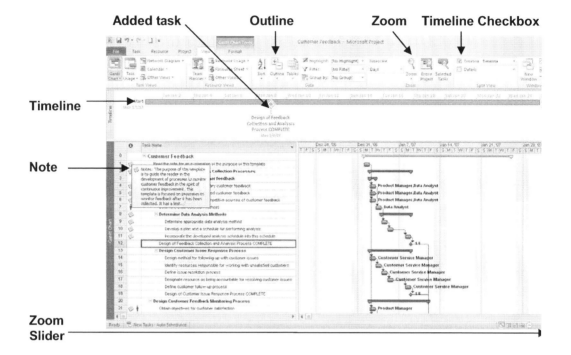

Figure A-7. Adjusted Customer Feedback.mpp file

To show different WBS levels:

1. Select Outline Level 1 to display WBS level 2 tasks. Click the **Outline** button's list arrow, and then click **Outline Level 1**. Notice that only the level 2 WBS items display in the Entry table. The black bars on the Gantt chart represent the summary tasks. Recall that the entire project is normally referred to as WBS level 1, and the next highest level is called level 2. This view of the file also shows one milestone task in row 45 indicating when the project was completed. Recall that the black diamond symbol on a Gantt chart shows milestones.

2. Expand a task. Click the **expand symbol** (the plus sign) to the left of Task 2, Develop Customer Feedback Collection Processes, to see its subtasks. Your screen should resemble Figure A-8. Click the **collapse symbol** (the minus sign) to hide its subtasks. Experiment with expanding and collapsing other tasks and resizing other columns.

Summary Task   **Milestone**

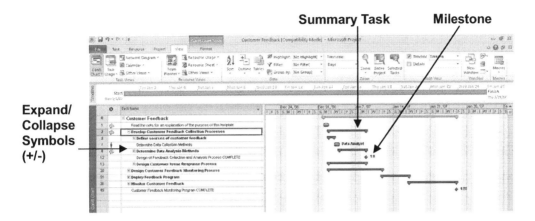

**Expand/
Collapse
Symbols
(+/-)**

Figure A-8. Showing part of the WBS on the Gantt chart

    3. Close the file without saving. Click the **Close icon** in the upper right of the window and select **No** when prompted to save the file.

Project 2010 Views

Project 2010 provides many ways to display or view project information. In addition to the default Gantt chart, you can view the network diagram, calendar, and task usage views, to name a few. These views allow you to analyze project information in different ways. The View tab also provides access to different tables that display information in various ways. In addition to the default Entry table view, you can access tables that focus on data related to areas such as the Schedule, Cost, Tracking, and Earned Value.

    To access and explore different views:

    1. Explore the Network Diagram view in the Customer Feedback file. Open the Customer Feedback file again. Click the **Network Diagram** button under the View tab, and then move the **Zoom slider** on the lower right of the screen all the way to the left. Your screen should resemble Figure A-9.

Network Diagram View   **Zoom Slider**

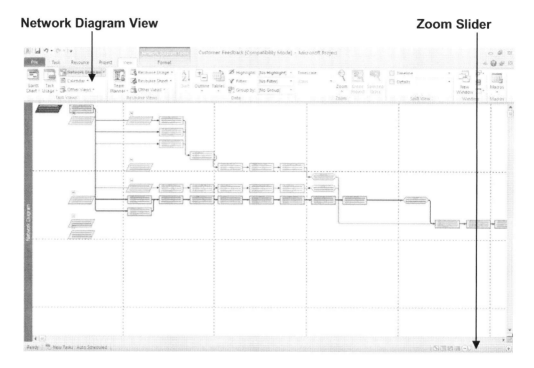

Figure A-9. Network diagram view of customer feedback file

2. *Explore the Calendar view.* Click the **Calendar** button (under the Network Diagram button). Notice that the screen lists tasks each day in a calendar format.

3. *Examine columns in the Entry table.* Click the **Gantt Chart** button, move the split bar to the right to see all of the available columns, and review the information provided in each column of the Entry table.

4. *Change the table view.* Click the **Tables** button under the View tab, and then click **Schedule**. Figure A-10 shows the table view options.

Figure A-10. Table view options

5. *Examine the Table: Schedule and other views*. Notice that the columns in the table to the left of the Gantt chart, as shown in Figure A-11, now display more detailed schedule information, such as Task Mode, Task Name, Start, Finish, Late Start, Late Finish, Free Slack, and Total Slack. Also notice that all of the text in the Task Name column is not visible. Remember that you can widen the column by double-clicking the resize pointer to the right of that column. You can also move the split bar to reveal more or fewer columns. Experiment with other table views, then **return to the Table: Entry view**.

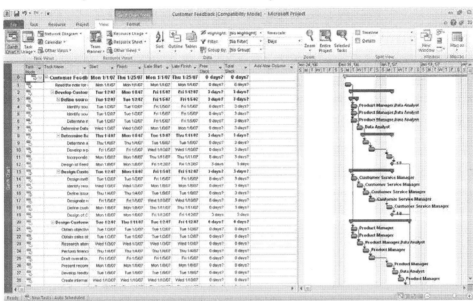

Figure A-11. Schedule table view

Project 2010 Reports

Project 2010 provides many ways to report project information as well. In addition to traditional reports, you can also prepare visual reports, with both available under the Project tab. Note that the visual reports often require that you have other Microsoft application software, such as Excel and Visio. Project 2010 automatically formats reports for ease of printing.

To access and explore different reports:

1. *Explore the Reports feature*. Click the **Project** tab, and then click the **Reports** button. The Reports dialog box displays, as shown in Figure A-12.

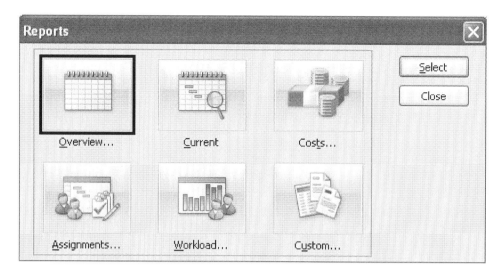

Figure A-12. Reports dialog box

> 2. *View the Project Summary report.* Double-click **Overview** from the Reports dialog box, and then double-click **Project Summary** in the Overview Reports dialog box. Notice that Project 2010 switches to the Backstage (File tab) to make it easy for you to print or share your report, as shown in Figure A-13.

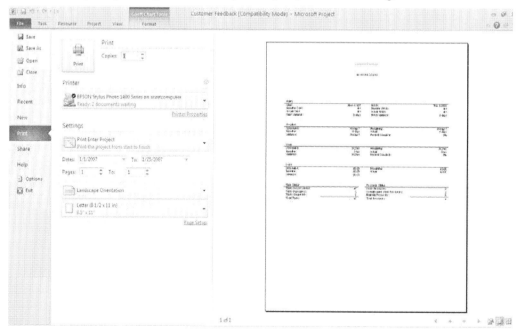

Figure A-13. Previewing the Project Summary report in the Backstage

> 3. *Examine the report and experiment with others.* Move the mouse to the right side of the screen to exam the report more closely. Notice that the insertion point

now resembles a magnifying glass. Click inside the report to zoom in or zoom out. Click the **Project** tab again, and then experiment with viewing other reports. You will use several reports and other views later in this appendix.

4.   *Close the Reports feature.* Click **Project** tab to return to the Gantt chart view. You can close the file without saving it if you wish to take a break.

Project 2010 Filters

Project 2010 uses a relational database to filter, sort, store, and display information. Filtering project information is very useful. For example, if a project includes thousands of tasks, you might want to view only summary or milestone tasks to get a high-level view of the project by using the Milestones or Summary Tasks filter from the Filter list. You can select a filter that shows only tasks on the critical path if that is what you want to see. Other filters include Completed Tasks, Late/Overbudget Tasks, and Date Range, which displays tasks based on dates you provide. As shown earlier, you can also click the Show button on the toolbar to display different levels in the WBS quickly.

To explore Project 2010 filters:

1.   *Access filters.* Click the **View** tab, if necessary, and make sure the Customer Feedback file is in the Gantt Chart: Table Entry view. Click the **Filter list arrow** (under the Data group), as shown in Figure A-14. The default filter is No Filter, which shows all tasks.

Filter list arrow

Figure A-14. Using a filter

> 2. *Filter to show critical tasks.* Click **Critical** in the list of filters. Widen the Task Names column, if needed, and move the split bar to see only that column. Notice that the Gantt chart only shows the critical tasks for the project. Your screen should resemble Figure A-15. Recall that the critical tasks are what drive the schedule completion date.

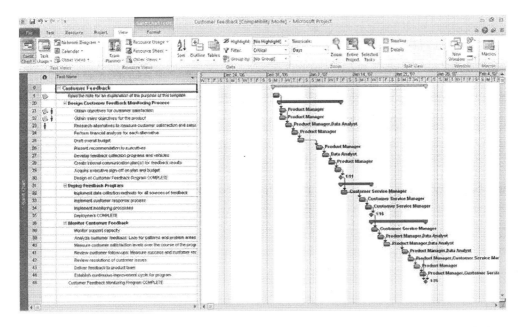

Figure A-15. Critical tasks filter applied

3. *Show summary tasks*. Select **No Filter** from the Filter list box to reveal all the tasks in the WBS again. Click the **Filter** list arrow, and then click **Summary Tasks**. Now only the summary tasks appear in the WBS. Experiment with other filters.

4. *Close the file*. When you are finished reviewing the Customer Feedback file, click **Close** from the File menu or click the **Close** button. Click **No** when asked if you want to save changes.

5. *Exit Project 2010*. Select **Exit** from the File tab or click the **Close** button for Project 2010.

Now that you are familiar with the main screen elements, views, reports, and filters, you will learn how to use Project 2010 to create a new file.

CREATING A NEW FILE AND ENTERING TASKS IN A WORK BREAKDOWN STRUCTURE

To create a new Project 2010 file, you must first name the project, enter the start date, and then enter the tasks. The list of tasks and their hierarchy is the work breakdown structure (WBS). The file you create could be used for a class project which lasts approximately three months. It uses the project management process groups to organize tasks and includes several deliverables described in this text. You could also modify this file to meet your specific needs.

NOTE: In this section, you will go through several steps to create a new Project 2010 file named wbs.mpp. If you want to download the completed file to check your work or continue to the next section, a copy of wbs.mpp is available on the companion Web site for this text at www.intropm.com. Try to complete an entire section of this appendix (entering tasks in a work breakdown structure, developing the schedule, and so on) in one sitting to create the complete file.

Creating a New Project File

To create a new project file:

1. *Create a blank project.* Open Project 2010. A blank project file automatically opens. The default filenames are Project1, Project2, and so on. (If Project 2010 is already open and you want to open a new file, click the **File** tab and select a **Blank Project**.)

2. *Open the Project Information dialog box.* Click the **Project** tab, and then click **Project Information** to display the Project Information dialog box, as shown in Figure A-16. This dialog box enables you to set dates for the project, select the calendar to use, and view project statistics. The project start date will default to the current date. Note that in Figure A-16 the file was created on 2/24/10 and a Start date of 2/1/10 was entered.

NOTE: All dates are entered in month/day/year or American format. You can change the date format by selecting Options from the File tab. Click the date format you want to use in the Date Format box under the General settings. You can also customize the Ribbon, change default currencies in the display, and so on under Project Options.

Start date text box

Current date

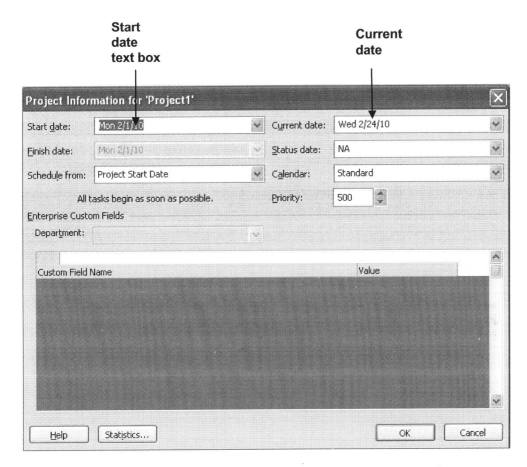

Figure A-16. Project information dialog box

3. *Enter the project start date.* In the Start date text box, enter **2/01/10**. Setting your project start date to 2/01/10 will ensure that your work matches the results that appear in this appendix. Leave the Finish date, Current date, and other information at the default settings. Click **OK** or press Enter.

4. *Access advanced project properties.* Click the **File** tab, and then click **Info**. Click Project Information on the right side of the screen to access Advanced Properties, as shown in Figure A-17.

Advanced Properties

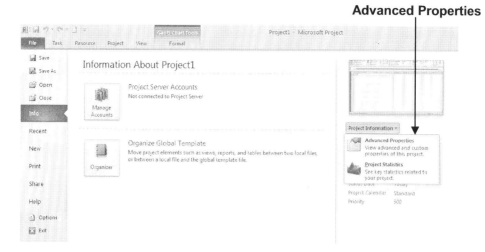

Figure A-17. Accessing advanced project properties

5. *Enter advanced project properties* Type **Project A+** in the Title text box, type **Your Name** in the Author text box, as shown in Figure A-18, and then click **OK**. You may have some default information entered in the Project Properties dialog box, such as your company's name. Click the **Task** tab so you can see the Entry table and Gantt chart view. Keep this file open for the next set of steps.

Figure A-18. Project properties dialog box

Creating a Work Breakdown Structure Hierarchy

As mentioned in Chapter 4 of this text, a work breakdown structure (WBS) is a fundamental part of project management. Developing a good WBS takes time, and it will make entering tasks into the Entry table easier if you develop the WBS first. For this example, you will use the project management process groups and some key processes and deliverables to create the WBS. You will use the information in Figure A-19 to enter tasks.

1. Initiating	16. Work on deliverable 2
2. Identify stakeholders	17. Work on deliverable 3
3. Stakeholder register completed	18. Deliverable 1 completed
4. Stakeholder management strategy completed	19. Deliverable 2 completed
5. Prepare project charter	20. Deliverable 3 completed
6. Project charter completed	21. Monitoring and Controlling
7. Prepare for kickoff meeting	22. Track actual hours
8. Kickoff meeting completed	23. Update project documents
9. Planning	24. Progress report 1
10. Prepare draft schedule	25. Progress report 2
11. Gantt chart completed	26. Hold meetings
12. Prepare scope statement	27. Closing
13. Initial scope statement completed	28. Prepare final project report
14. Executing	29. Prepare final presentation
15. Work on deliverable 1	30. Project completed

Figure A-19. Task list for Project A+

To develop a WBS for the project:

1. Enter task names. Enter the 30 tasks in Figure A-19 into the Task Name column in the order shown. Do not worry about durations or any other information at this time. Type the name of each task into the Task Name column of the Entry table, beginning with the first row. Press **Enter** or the **down arrow** key on your keyboard to move to the next row.

HELP: If you accidentally skip a task, highlight the task row, right-click, and select Insert Task. To edit a task entry, click the text for that task, and either type over the old text or edit the existing text.

> **TIP:** Entering tasks into Project 2010 and editing the information is similar to entering and editing data in an Excel spreadsheet. You can also easily copy and paste text from Excel or Word into Project, such as the list of tasks.

2. *Adjust the Task Name column width as needed.* To make all the text display in the Task Name column, move the mouse over the right-column gridline in the **Task Name** column heading until you see the resize pointer , and then click the **left mouse** button and drag the line to the right to make the column wider, or double-click to adjust the column width automatically.

This WBS separates tasks according to the project management process groups of initiating, planning, executing, controlling, and closing. These tasks will be the level 2 items in the WBS for this project. (Remember the whole project is level 1.) It is a good idea to include all of these process groups because there are important tasks that must be done under each of them. Recall that the WBS should include *all* of the work required for the project. In the Project A+ WBS, the tasks will be purposefully left at a high WBS level (level 3). You will create these levels, or the WBS hierarchy, next when you create summary tasks. For a real project, you would usually break the WBS into even more levels to provide more details to describe all the work involved in the project. For example, each deliverable would probably have several levels and tasks under it.

Creating Summary Tasks

After entering the WBS tasks listed in Figure A-19 into the Entry table, the next step is to show the WBS levels by creating summary tasks. The summary tasks in this example are Tasks 1 (initiating), 9 (planning), 14 (executing), 21 (monitoring and controlling), and 27 (closing). You create summary tasks by highlighting and indenting their respective subtasks.

To create the summary tasks:

1. *Select lower level or subtasks.* Highlight **Tasks 2** through **8** by clicking the cell for Task 2 and dragging the mouse through the cells to Task 8.

2. *Indent subtasks.* Click the **Indent Tasks** button on the Ribbon under the Schedule group of the Task tab (or press Alt + Shift + right arrow) so your screen resembles Figure A-19. After the subtasks (Tasks 2 through 8) are indented, notice that Task 1 automatically becomes boldface, which indicates that it is a summary task. A collapse symbol appears to the left of the new summary task name. Clicking the collapse symbol (minus sign) will collapse the summary task and hide the subtasks beneath it. When subtasks are hidden, an expand symbol (plus sign) appears to the left of the summary task name. Clicking the expand symbol will expand the summary task. Also, notice that the symbol for the summary task on the Gantt chart has changed from a blue to a black line with arrows indicating the start and end dates. The Task Mode has also changed to make this task Automatically scheduled. You'll learn more about this feature later. For now, focus on entering and indenting the tasks to create the WBS.

Expand or collapse symbols by Summary tasks

Indent Task

Summary task symbol

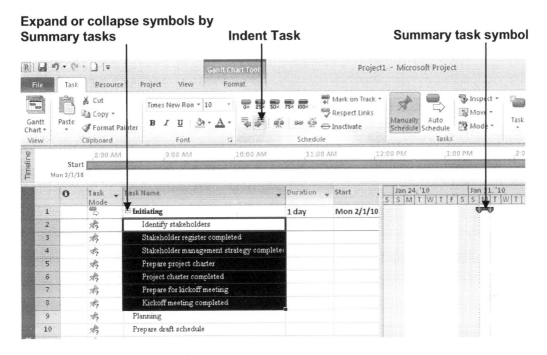

Figure A-19. Indenting tasks to create the WBS hierarchy

3. *Create other summary tasks and subtasks.* Create subtasks and summary tasks for the other process groups by following the same steps. Indent **Tasks 10** through **13** to make Task 9 a summary task. Indent **Tasks 15** through **20** to make Task 14 a summary task. Indent **Tasks 22** through **26** to make Task 21 a summary task. Indent **Tasks 28** through **30** to make Task 27 a summary task. Widen the Task Name column to see all of your text, as needed.

TIP: To change a task from a subtask to a summary task or to change its level in the WBS, you can "outdent" the task. To outdent the task, click the cell of the task or tasks you want to change, and then click the Outdent Task button (the button just to the left of the Indent Task button). You can also press Alt + Shift + Right Arrow to indent tasks and Alt + Shift + Left Arrow to outdent tasks.

Numbering Tasks

To display automatic numbering of tasks using the standard tabular numbering system for a WBS:

1. *Show outline numbers*. Click the **Format** tab, and then click the **Outline Number checkbox** under the Show/Hide group. Project 2010 adds the appropriate WBS numbering to the task names.

2. *Show project summary task*. Click the Project Summary checkbox just below the Outline Number checkbox. Scroll to the top of the file to see that a new task has been added under row 0.

3. *Adjust the file*. Widen the Task Name column and move the split bar so only that column displays. Your file should resemble Figure A-20.

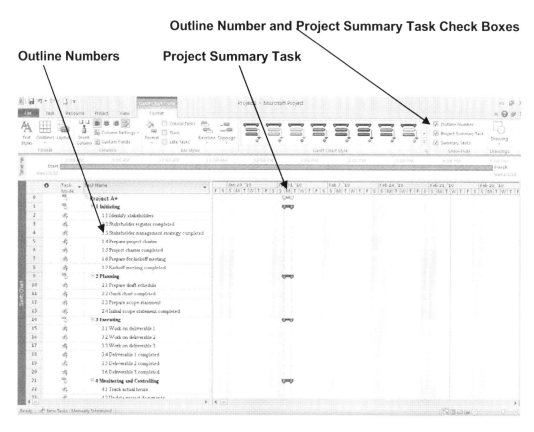

Figure A-20. Adding automatic outline numbers and a project summary task

Saving Project Files Without a Baseline

An important part of project management is tracking performance against a baseline, or approved plan. It is important to wait until you are ready to save your file with a baseline because Project 2010 will show changes against a baseline. Since you are still developing your project file for the Project A+ project, you want to save the file without a baseline, which is the default way to save a file. Later in this appendix, you will save the file with a baseline. You will then enter actual information to compare planned and actual performance data.

To save a file without a baseline:

1. Save your file. Click the **File** tab and then click **Save**, or click the **Save** button on the Quick Access toolbar.

2. Enter a filename. In the Save dialog box, type **wbs** in the File name text box. Browse to the location in which you want to save the file, and then click **Save**. Your Project 2010 file should look like Figure A-21. Remember that you can move the Split bar to show more or fewer columns.

3. Close Project 2010. Click the Close icon to exit Project 2010.

HELP: If you want to download the Project 2010 file wbs.mpp to check your work or continue to the next section, a copy is available on the companion Web site for this text, the author's Web site, or from your instructor.

28

Figure A-21. Project 2010 WBS file

DEVELOPING THE SCHEDULE

Many people use Project 2010 for its scheduling features. The first step in using these features, after inputting the WBS for the project, is to change calendars, if needed, and then enter durations for tasks or specific dates when tasks will occur. You must also enter task dependencies in order for schedules to adjust automatically and to do critical path analysis. After entering durations and task dependencies, you can view the network diagram, critical path, and slack information.

Calendars

The standard Project 2010 calendar assumes that working hours are Monday through Friday, from 8:00 a.m. to 5:00 p.m., with an hour for lunch from noon until 1:00 p.m. In addition to the standard calendar, Project 2010 also includes a 24 Hours calendar and Night Shift calendar. The 24 Hours calendar assumes resources can work any hour and any day of the week. The Night Shift calendar assumes working hours are Monday through Saturday, from 12:00 a.m. to 3:00 a.m., 4:00 a.m. 8 a.m., and 11 p.m. to 12 a.m. You can create a different base calendar to meet your unique project requirements.

To create a new base calendar:

1. *Open a new file and access the Change Working Time dialog box*. With Project 2010 open, click the **Project** tab, and then click the **Change Working Time** button under the Properties group. The Change Working Time dialog box opens, as shown in Figure A-22.

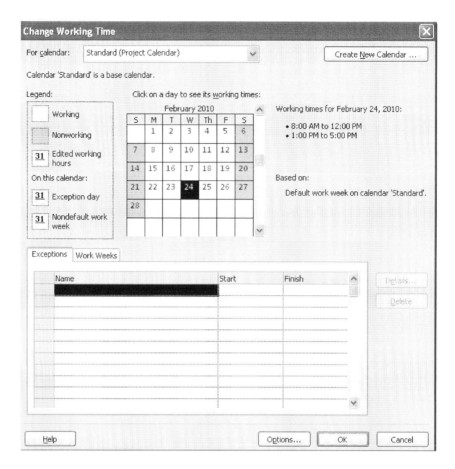

Figure A-22. Change Working Time dialog box

2. *Name the new base calendar*. In the Change Working Time dialog box, click **Create New Calendar**. The Create New Base Calendar dialog box opens. Click the **Create new base calendar** radio button, type **Project A+** as the name of the new calendar in the **Name** text box, and then click **OK**.

3. *Change the fiscal year start*. In the Change Working Time dialog box, click **Options** at the bottom of the screen. Change the **fiscal year** to start in **October** instead of January. Review other options in this screen, and then click **OK twice**.

You can use this new calendar for the whole project, or you can assign it to specific resources on the project.

To assign the new calendar to the whole project:

1. *Open the Project Information dialog box*. Click the **Project** tab, and then click the **Change Working Time** button.

2. *Select a new calendar.* Click the **For calendar** list arrow to display a list of available calendars. Select your new calendar named **Project A+** from this list, and then click **OK**.

To assign a specific calendar to a specific resource:

1. *Assign a new calendar.* Click the **View** tab, and then click the **Resource Sheet** button under the Resource Views group. Type **Adam** in the Resource Name column, press **Enter**, and then select the word **Adam**.

2. *Select the calendar.* Click the **Base Calendar** cell on the right part of the screen for Adam. If the Base Calendar column is not visible, click the horizontal scroll bar to view more columns. Click the **Base Calendar** list arrow to display the options, and then select **Project A+**, as shown in Figure A-23.

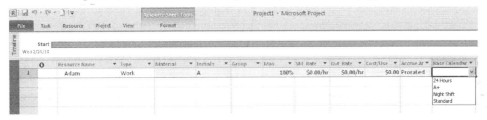

Figure A-23. Changing calendars for specific resources

3. *Block off vacation time.* Double-click the resource name **Adam** to display the Resource Information dialog box, and then click the **Change Working Time** button, located on the General tab in the Resource Information dialog box. You can block off vacation time for people by selecting the appropriate days on the calendar and marking them as nonworking days. Click **OK** to accept your changes, and then click **OK** to close the Resource Information dialog box.

4. *Close the file without saving it.* Click the **Close** box, and then click **No** when you are prompted to save the file.

Entering Task Durations

Recall that duration includes the actual amount of time spent working on a task plus elapsed time. Duration does not equal effort. For example, you might have a task that you estimate will take one person 40 hours of effort to complete, but you allow two weeks on a calendar for its duration. You can simply enter 2w (for two weeks) in the Duration column for that task

Manual and Automatic Scheduling

If you have used earlier versions of Project, you probably noticed that when you entered a task, it was automatically assigned a duration of one day, and Start and Finish dates were also automatically entered. This is still the case in Project 2010 if you use automatic scheduling for a task. If you use manual scheduling, no durations or dates are automatically entered. The other big change with manual scheduling is that summary task durations are not automatically calculated based on their subtasks when they are set up as manually scheduled tasks. Figure A-24 illustrates these differences. Notice that the Manual subtask 1 had no information entered for its duration, start, or finish dates. Also note that the duration for Manual summary task 1's duration is not dependent on the durations of its subtasks. For the automatic summary task, its duration is dependent on its summary tasks, and information is entered for all of the durations, start, and end dates. You can switch between automatic and manual scheduling for tasks in the same file, as desired, by changing the Task Mode.

Task Mode	Task Name	Duration	Start	Finish
	⊟ Manual summary task 1	4 wks	Thu 2/25/10	Wed 3/24/10
	Manual subtask 1			
	Manual subtask 2	2 wks		
	⊟ Automatic summary task 1	15 days	Thu 2/25/10	Wed 3/17/10
	Automatic subtask 1	1 wk	Thu 2/25/10	Wed 3/3/10
	Automatic subtask 2	2 wks	Thu 3/4/10	Wed 3/17/10

Figure A-24. Manual versus automatic scheduling

When you move your mouse over the Task Mode column (shown in the far left in Figure A-24) Project 2010 displays the following information:

- A task can be with Manually Scheduled or Automatically Scheduled.
- Manually Scheduled tasks have user-defined Start, Finish and Duration values. Project will never change their dates, but may warn you if there are potential issues with the entered values.
- Automatically Scheduled tasks have Start, Finish and Duration values calculated by Project based on dependencies, constraints, calendars, and other factors.

Project Help provides the following example of using both manual and automatic scheduling. You set up a preliminary project plan that's still in the proposal stage. You have a vague idea of major milestone dates but not much detail on other dates in various phases of the project. You build tasks and milestones using the Manually Scheduled task mode. The proposal is accepted and the tasks and deliverable dates become more defined. You continue to manually schedule those tasks and dates for a while, but as certain phases become well-defined, you decide to switch the tasks in those phases to the Automatically Scheduled task mode. By letting Project 2010 handle the complexities of scheduling, you can focus your attention on those phases that are still under development.

Duration Units and Guidelines for Entering Durations

To indicate the length of a task's duration, you normally type both a number and an appropriate duration symbol. If you type only a number, Project 2010 automatically enters days as the duration unit. Duration unit symbols include:

- d = days (default)

- w = weeks

- m = minutes

- h = hours

- mo or mon = months

- ed = elapsed days

- ew = elapsed weeks

For example, to enter two weeks for a task's duration, type 2w in the Duration column. (You can also type wk, wks, week, or weeks, instead of just w.) To enter four days for a task's duration, type 4 or 4d in the Duration column. You can also enter elapsed times in the Duration column. For example, 3ed means three elapsed days, and 2ew means two elapsed weeks.

You would use an elapsed duration for a task like "Allow cement to dry." The cement will dry in exactly the same amount of time regardless of whether it is a workday, a weekend, or a holiday. Project's default calendar does not assume that work is done on weekends. You will learn to change the calendar later in this appendix.

It is important to follow a few important rules when entering durations:

- To mark a task as a milestone, enter 0 for the duration. You can also mark tasks that have a non-zero duration as milestones by checking the "Mark task as milestone" option in the Task Information dialog box on the Advanced tab. You simply double-click a task to access this dialog box. The milestone symbol for those tasks will appear at their start date.

- You can enter the exact start and finish dates for activities instead of entering durations in the automatic scheduling mode. To enter start and finish dates, move the split bar to the right to reveal the Start and Finish columns. You normally only enter start and finish dates in this mode when those dates are certain.

- If you want task dates to adjust according to any other task dates, do not enter exact start and finish dates. Instead, enter durations and then establish dependencies to related tasks.

- To enter recurring tasks, such as weekly meetings, select Recurring Task from the Task button under the Task tab, Insert group. Enter the task name, the duration, and when the task occurs. Project 2010 will automatically insert appropriate subtasks based on the length of the project and the number of tasks required for the recurring task.

- Project 2010 uses a default calendar with standard workdays and hours. Remember to change the default calendar if needed, as shown earlier.

Next, you will set task durations in the **Project A+** file that you created and saved in the previous section. If you did not create the file named wbs.mpp, you can download it from the companion Web site for this text.

Use the information in Figure A-25 to enter durations. The Project 2010 row number is shown to the left of each task name in the table.

Task Row	Task Name	Duration
2	Identify stakeholders	1w
3	Stakeholder register completed	0
4	Stakeholder management strategy completed	0
5	Prepare project charter	1w
6	Project charter completed	0
7	Prepare for kickoff meeting	3d
8	Kickoff meeting completed	0
10	Prepare draft schedule	5d
11	Gantt chart completed	0
12	Prepare scope statement	8d
13	Initial scope statement completed	0
15	Work on deliverable 1	3w
16	Work on deliverable 2	5w
17	Work on deliverable 3	6w
18	Deliverable 1 completed	0
19	Deliverable 2 completed	0
20	Deliverable 3 completed	0
24	Progress report 1	0
25	Progress report 2	0
28	Prepare final project report	4d
29	Prepare final presentation	4d
30	Project completed	0

Figure A-25. Task durations for Project A+

Entering Task Durations

To enter task durations:

1. *Enter the duration for Task 2*. Open the wbs file, and move the split bar to the right, if needed, to reveal the Duration, Start, and Finish columns. Click the **Duration** column for row 2, Identify stakeholders, type **1w**, and then press **Enter**. Notice that the duration for the first task, Initiating, also changed since it is a summary task and is an Automatically scheduled task, as shown in the Task Mode column. When you created summary tasks earlier, Project changed their scheduling mode to Automatic. Also notice that the Start and Finish date for Task 2 remain blank, since that task is a Manually scheduled task.

2. *Enter the duration for Task 3* In the **Duration** column for row 3, Stakeholder register completed, type **0**, then press **Enter**. Remember that a task with zero duration is a milestone. Notice the milestone or black diamond symbol that appears on the Gantt chart, as shown in Figure A-26

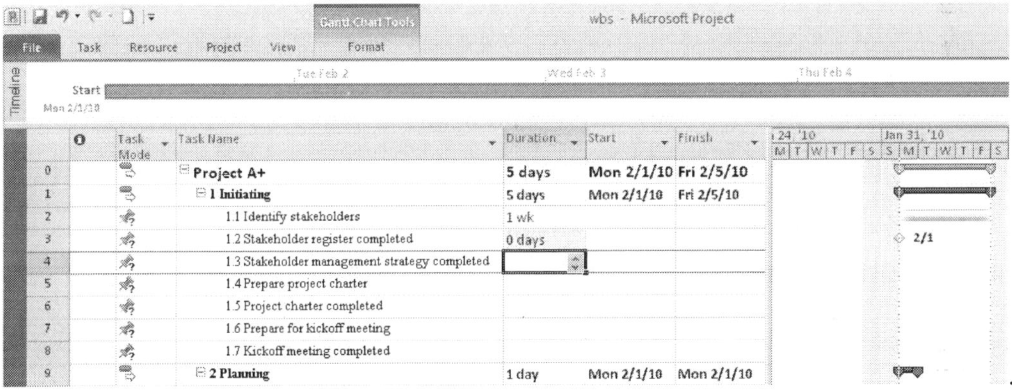

Figure A-26. Entering task durations

3. *Make all tasks Automatically scheduled tasks*. To save time since you do want most of the tasks to be automatically scheduled, select all of the tasks by clicking the **Task Name** column heading, and then click the **Auto Schedule** button under the **Task** tab, Tasks group.

4. *Enter remaining task durations*. Continue to enter the durations using the information in Figure A-25. Do not enter durations for tasks not listed in the figure. Notice that the Planning Wizard dialog box displays when you make the same entry several times in a row, such as after task 20. Click OK to close the dialog box.

5. *Insert a recurring task above Task 26, Hold meetings.* Click **Hold meetings** (Task 26) in the Task Name column to select that task. Click the **Task** tab, and click the **Task** button drop-down box under the Insert group, and then click **Recurring Task**. The Recurring Task Information dialog box opens.

6. *Enter task and duration information for the recurring task.* Type **Hold meetings** as the task title in the Task Name text box. Type **30min** in the Duration text box. Select the **Weekly** radio button under Recurrence pattern. Make sure that **1** is entered in the **Recur every** list box. Select the **Thursday** check box. In the Range of recurrence section, type **2/1/10** in the Start text box, click the **End by** radio button, and then type **4/29/10** in the End by text box, as shown in Figure A-27. The new recurring task will appear above Task 26, Hold meetings, when you are finished. **Delete task 40**, Hold meetings, by right clicking anywhere in row 40 and selecting Delete Task.

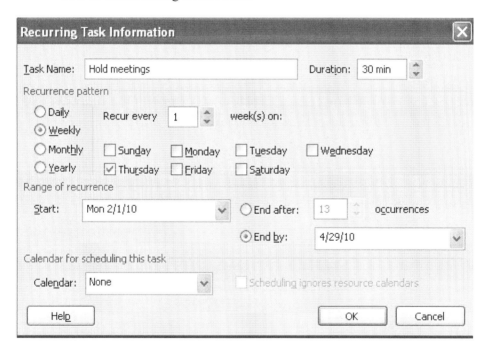

Figure A-27. Recurring task information dialog box

TIP: You can also enter a number of occurrences instead of an End by date for a recurring task. You might need to adjust the End by date after you enter all of your task durations and dependencies. Remember, the date on your computer determines the date listed as Today in the calendar.

7. *View the new summary task and its subtasks.* Click **OK**. Project 2010 inserts a new Hold meetings subtask in the Task Name column. Expand the new subtask

by clicking the **expand symbol** to the left of Hold meetings. To collapse the recurring task, click the **collapse symbol.** Move your mouse over the Recurring Task symbol in the Indicator column for row 26. Notice that the recurring task appears on the appropriate dates on the Gantt chart.

8. *Adjust the columns displayed and the timescale.* Move the **split bar** so that only the Task Name and Duration columns are visible. If needed, increase the Duration column's width so all of the text is visible. Click the **Zoom Out** button on the Zoom slider in the lower left of the screen to display all of the symbols in the Gantt chart. Your screen should resemble Figure A-28.

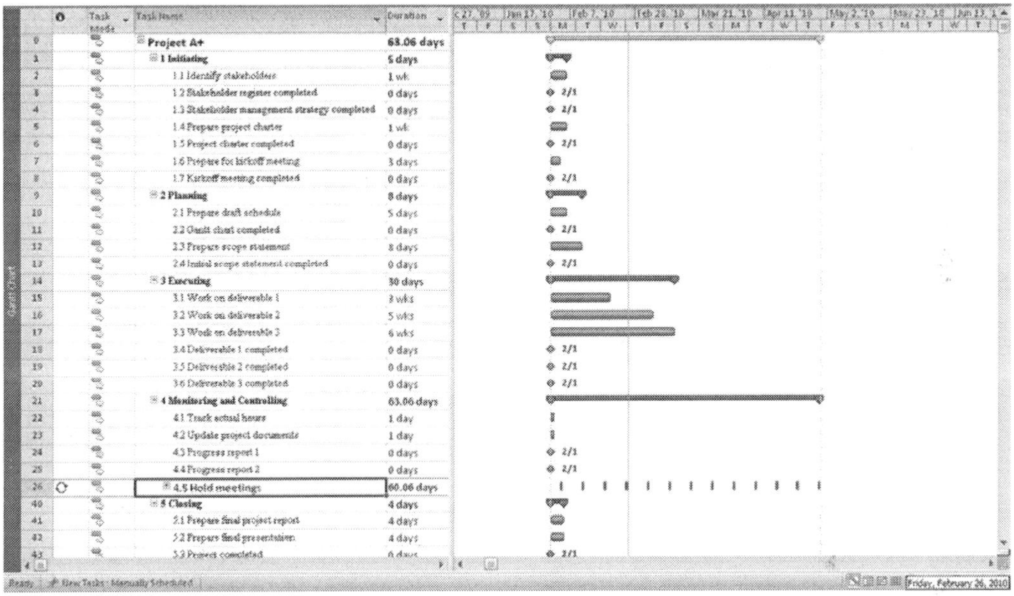

Figure A-28. All task durations and recurring task entered

9. *Save your file and name it.* Click **File** on the Menu bar, and then click **Save As**. Enter **schedule** as the filename, and then save the file to the desired location on your computer or network. Notice that all of the tasks still begin on February 1. This will change when you add task dependencies. Keep this file open for the next set of steps.

Establishing Task Dependencies

To use Project 2010 to adjust schedules automatically and perform critical path analysis, you *must* determine the dependencies or relationships among tasks. There are several different methods for creating task dependencies: using the Link Tasks button, using the Predecessors column of the Entry table or the Predecessors tab in the Task Information dialog box, or clicking and dragging the Gantt chart symbols for tasks with dependencies. You will use the first two methods in the following steps.

To create dependencies using the Link Tasks button, highlight tasks that are related and then click the Link Tasks button under the Task tab, Schedule group. For example, to create a finish-to-start (FS) dependency between Task 1 and Task 2, click any cell in row 1, drag down to row 2, and then click the Link Tasks button. The default type of link is finish-to-start. In the Project A+ file, you will also set up some other types of dependencies and use the lag option to set up overlaps between dependent tasks.

TIP: To select adjacent tasks, click and drag the mouse to highlight them. You can also click the first task, hold down the Shift key, and then click the last task. To select nonadjacent tasks, hold down the Control (Ctrl) key as you click tasks in order of their dependencies.

When you use the Predecessors column of the Entry table to create dependencies, you must manually enter the information. To create dependencies manually, type the task row number of the preceding task in the Predecessors column of the Entry table. For example, Task 3 has Task 2 as a predecessor, which can be entered in the Predecessors column, meaning that Task 3 cannot start until Task 2 is finished. To see the Predecessors column of the Entry table, move the split bar to the right. You can also double-click on the task, click the Predecessors tab in the Task Information dialog box, and enter the predecessors there.

Next, you will use information from Figure A-29 to enter the predecessors for tasks as indicated. You will create some dependencies by manually typing the predecessors in the Predecessors column, some by using the Link Tasks button, and the remaining dependencies by using whichever method you prefer.

To link tasks or establish dependencies for Project A+:

1. Display the Predecessors column in the Entry table. Move the split bar to the right to reveal the full Predecessors column in the schedule.mpp file you saved in the previous section. Widen the Task Name or other columns, if needed.

2. Highlight the cell where you want to enter a predecessor, and then type the task number for its predecessor task. Click the **Predecessors cell for Task 3**, Stakeholder register completed, type **2**, and press **Enter**. Notice that as you enter task dependencies, the Gantt chart changes to reflect the new schedule. Also notice that several cells become highlighted, showing the Visual Change Highlights feature of Project 2010.

3. Enter predecessors for Task 4. Click the **Predecessors cell** for Task 4, type **2**, and press **Enter**.

4. Establish dependencies using the Link Tasks button. To link Tasks 5 and 6, click the task name for Task 5 in the Task Name column and drag down through Task 6. Then, click the Task Tab, and click the **Link Tasks** button (looks like a chain link) under the Schedule group. Notice that the result is the same as typing 5 in the Predecessors column for Task 6.

5. *Enter dependencies and lag time using the Task Information dialog box.*
Double-click on the **Task Name** for **task 5**, Prepare project charter, and then
click on the **Predecessors tab** in the Task Information dialog box. Click in the
cell under Task Name, and then click the **Task Name** down arrow and select
Identify stakeholders. Click the **Type** drop down arrow to see the various types
of dependencies. For this task, you will keep the default type of finish-to-start.
Click the **Lag drop down arrow**, then **type -50%** and press **Enter**. (Lag means
there is a gap between tasks, and lead or negative lag means there is an overlap).
Your screen should resemble Figure A-29. Click **OK** to close the dialog box.
Notice that the Predecessor column for task 5 displays 2FS-50%, meaning there
is a finish-to-start relationship with task 2 and a lag of -50%, meaning the task
can start when task 2 is 50% completed.

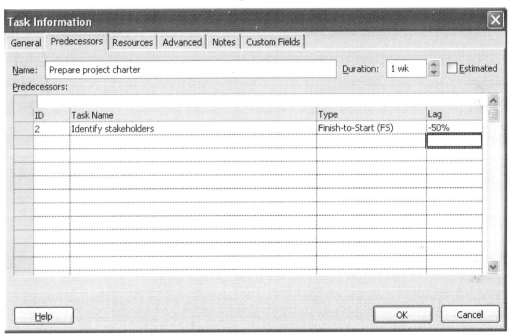

**Figure A-29. Entering predecessor information using the task information dialog
box**

6. *Enter remaining dependencies.* **Link the other tasks** by either manually
entering the predecessors into the Predecessors column, by using the Link Tasks
button, or using the Task Information dialog box. Use the information in Figure
A-30 to make your entries. If you have entered all data correctly, the project
should end on 4/30, or April 30, 2010. (Note that you could manually enter a
Start date for tasks 22 and 23 to make those dates more realistic. The current
dependency shows them both ending one day before the project ends.)

Task Row	Task Name	Predecessors
3	Stakeholder register completed	2
4	Stakeholder management strategy completed	2
5	Prepare project charter	2FS-50%
6	Project charter completed	5
7	Prepare for kickoff meeting	2,6
8	Kickoff meeting completed	6,7
10	Prepare draft schedule	5,12FS-50%
11	Gantt chart completed	10
12	Prepare scope statement	5
13	Initial scope statement completed	12
15	Work on deliverable 1	12
16	Work on deliverable 2	18
17	Work on deliverable 3	18
18	Deliverable 1 completed	15
19	Deliverable 2 completed	16
20	Deliverable 3 completed	17
22	Track actual hours	43FF-1 day,2
23	Update project documents	43FF-1 day,3
41	Prepare final project report	18,19,20
42	Prepare final presentation	18,19,20
43	Project completed	41,42

Figure A-30. Predecessor information for Project A+

7. *Review the file.* If needed, click the **Zoom Out** button on the Zoom slider to adjust the timescale so all of the information shows on your screen. When you finish, your screen should resemble Figure A-31. Double-check your screen to make sure you entered the dependencies correctly.

	Task Mode	Task Name	Duration	Start	Finish	Predecessors
0		⊟ Project A+	64.5 days	Mon 2/1/10	Fri 4/30/10	
1		⊟ 1 Initiating	10.5 days	Mon 2/1/10	Mon 2/15/10	
2		1.1 Identify stakeholders	1 wk	Mon 2/1/10	Fri 2/5/10	
3		1.2 Stakeholder register completed	0 days	Fri 2/5/10	Fri 2/5/10	2
4		1.3 Stakeholder management strategy completed	0 days	Fri 2/5/10	Fri 2/5/10	2
5		1.4 Prepare project charter	1 wk	Wed 2/3/10	Wed 2/10/10	2FS-50%
6		1.5 Project charter completed	0 days	Wed 2/10/10	Wed 2/10/10	5
7		1.6 Prepare for kickoff meeting	3 days	Wed 2/10/10	Mon 2/15/10	2,6
8		1.7 Kickoff meeting completed	0 days	Mon 2/15/10	Mon 2/15/10	6,7
9		⊟ 2 Planning	9 days	Wed 2/10/10	Tue 2/23/10	
10		2.1 Prepare draft schedule	5 days	Tue 2/16/10	Tue 2/23/10	5,12FS-50%
11		2.2 Gantt chart completed	0 days	Tue 2/23/10	Tue 2/23/10	10
12		2.3 Prepare scope statement	8 days	Wed 2/10/10	Mon 2/22/10	5
13		2.4 Initial scope statement completed	0 days	Mon 2/22/10	Mon 2/22/10	12
14		⊟ 3 Executing	45 days	Mon 2/22/10	Mon 4/26/10	
15		3.1 Work on deliverable 1	3 wks	Mon 2/22/10	Mon 3/15/10	12
16		3.2 Work on deliverable 2	5 wks	Mon 3/15/10	Mon 4/19/10	18
17		3.3 Work on deliverable 3	6 wks	Mon 3/15/10	Mon 4/26/10	18
18		3.4 Deliverable 1 completed	0 days	Mon 3/15/10	Mon 3/15/10	15
19		3.5 Deliverable 2 completed	0 days	Mon 4/19/10	Mon 4/19/10	16
20		3.6 Deliverable 3 completed	0 days	Mon 4/26/10	Mon 4/26/10	17
21		⊟ 4 Monitoring and Controlling	63.5 days	Mon 2/1/10	Thu 4/29/10	
22		4.1 Track actual hours	1 day	Wed 4/28/10	Thu 4/29/10	43FF-1 day,2
23		4.2 Update project documents	1 day	Wed 4/28/10	Thu 4/29/10	43FF-1 day,3
24		4.3 Progress report 1	0 days	Mon 2/1/10	Mon 2/1/10	
25		4.4 Progress report 2	0 days	Mon 2/1/10	Mon 2/1/10	
26		⊞ 4.5 Hold meetings	60.06 days	Thu 2/4/10	Thu 4/29/10	
40		⊟ 5 Closing	4 days	Mon 4/26/10	Fri 4/30/10	
41		5.1 Prepare final project report	4 days	Mon 4/26/10	Fri 4/30/10	18,19,20
42		5.2 Prepare final presentation	4 days	Mon 4/26/10	Fri 4/30/10	18,19,20
43		5.3 Project completed	0 days	Fri 4/30/10	Fri 4/30/10	41,42

Figure A-31. Project A+ file with durations and dependencies entered

8. *Preview and save your file.* Click the **File** tab, and then select **Print** to preview and print your file, if desired. Make adjustments as needed back in the Task tab, and preview the file until it looks correct. When you are finished, **save** your schedule file again. Keep the file open for the next set of steps.

Gantt Charts, Network Diagrams, and Critical Path Analysis

Project 2010 shows a Gantt chart as the default view to the right of the Entry table. As described earlier in this text, network diagrams are often used to show task dependencies. This section explains important information about Gantt charts and network diagrams and describes how to make critical path information more visible in the Gantt Chart view.

Because you have already created task dependencies, you can now find the critical path for Project A+. You can view the critical tasks by changing the color of those items in the Gantt Chart view. Tasks on the critical path will automatically be red in the Network Diagram view. You can also view critical path information in the Schedule table or by using the Critical Tasks report.

To make the text for the critical path tasks appear in red on the Gantt chart:

1. Change the critical tasks format. Using the schedule.mpp file you previously saved, click the **Format** tab, and then click the Critical Tasks check box in the Bar Styles group, as shown in Figure A-32. Notice that the critical tasks display in red in the Gantt chart.

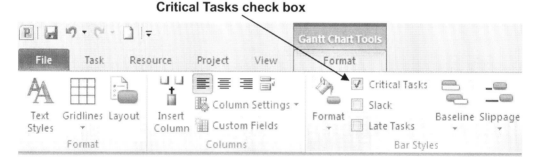

Figure A-32. Formatting critical tasks

2. View the network diagram. Click the View tab, and then click the **Network Diagram** button under the Task Views group Click the **Zoom Out** button on the Zoom slider several times and watch the view change. Figure A-30 shows all of the tasks in the Project A+ network diagram. Note that milestone tasks, such as Stakeholder management strategy completed, the fourth box on the top, appear as pointed rectangular boxes, while other tasks appear as rectangles. Move your mouse over that box to see it in a larger view. Notice that tasks on the critical path automatically appear in red. A dashed line on a network diagram represents a page break. You often need to change some of the default settings for the Network Diagram view before printing it. As you can see, network diagrams can be messy, so you might prefer to highlight critical tasks on the Gantt chart as you did earlier for easier viewing.

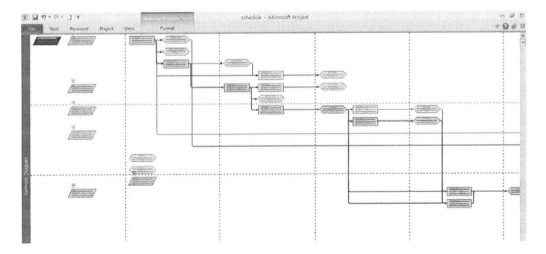

Figure A-34. Network diagram view

3. *View the schedule table.* Click the **Gantt Chart** button under the **View** tab to return to Gantt Chart view. Right-click the **Select All** button to the left of the Task Mode column heading and select **Schedule**. Alternatively, you can click the **View** tab and click the **Tables** button under the Data group and then select **Schedule**. The Schedule table replaces the Entry table to the left of the Gantt Chart. Your screen should resemble Figure A-35. This view shows the start and finish (meaning the early start and early finish) and late start and late finish dates for each task, as well as free and total slack. Right-click the **Select All** button and select **Entry** to return to the Entry table view.

Select All button   Schedule table

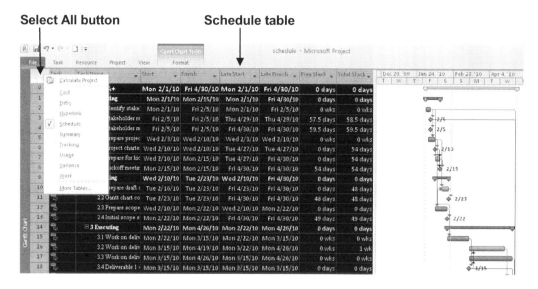

Figure A-35. Schedule table view

4.   *Open the Reports dialog box*. Click the **Project** tab, and then click the
Reports button under the Reports group. Double-click **Overview** to open the
Overview Reports dialog box, and then double-click **Critical Tasks**. A Critical
Tasks report as of today's date is displayed.

5.   *Close the report and save your file*. When you are finished examining the
Critical Tasks report, click the **Tasks**. Click the **Save** button on the Quick Access
toolbar to save your final schedule.mpp file, showing the Entry table and Gantt
chart view. Close Project 2010 if you are not continuing to the next section.

HELP: If you want to download the Project 2010 file schedule.mpp to check your work
or continue to the next section, a copy is available on the companion Web site for this
text at www.intropm.com.

Next you will explore some of the cost and resource management features of
Project 2010.

PROJECT COST AND RESOURCE MANAGEMENT

Many people do not use Project 2010 for cost or resource management. Most
organizations have more established cost management software products and procedures
in place, and many people simply do not know how to use the cost or resource
management features of Project 2010. However, these features make it possible to
integrate total project information more easily. This section offers brief instructions for
entering fixed and variable cost estimates, assigning resources to tasks, viewing resource
histograms, and entering actual cost and schedule information after establishing a
baseline plan. It also explains how to use Project 2010 for earned value management.

More details on these features are available in Project Help, online tutorials, or other texts. See other chapters of this text for information on some of these concepts.

Entering Fixed and Variable Cost Estimates

You can enter costs as fixed or variable. Fixed costs include costs like a specific quantity of materials or consultants hired at a fixed cost. Variable costs vary based on the amount of materials or hours people work. On many projects, human resource costs are the largest percentage of total project costs.

Entering Fixed Costs in the Cost Table

The Cost table allows you to easily enter fixed costs related to each task. You will enter a fixed cost of $200 related to Task 15, Work on deliverable 1.

To enter a fixed cost:

1. Display the Cost Table view. Open your Project 2010 file schedule.mpp, if necessary. Right-click the **Select All** button to the left of the Task Mode column heading and select **Cost**. The Cost table replaces the Entry table to the left of the Gantt chart. Widen the Task Name column and move the **split bar** to the right, as needed, until you see the entire Cost table. **Widen** the Task Name column to reveal all of the text in that column.

2. Enter a fixed cost. In the **Fixed Cost column for Task 15**, Work on deliverable 1, type **200** and press **Enter**. Notice that the Total Cost and Remaining Cost columns reflect this entry, and changes are made to the summary task, Executing, as well. Your screen should resemble Figure A-36

Select All button   **Fixed Cost column of cost table**

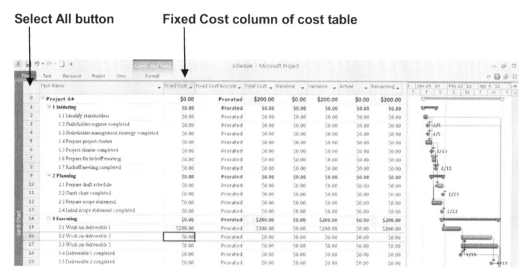

Figure A-36. Entering a fixed cost

Entering Resource Information and Cost Estimates

Several methods are available for entering resource information in Project 2010. The Resource Sheet allows you to enter the resource name, initials, resource group, maximum units, standard rate, overtime rate, cost/use, accrual method, base calendar, and code. Once you have established resources in the Resource Sheet, you can assign those resources to tasks in the Entry table with the list arrow that appears when you click a cell in the Resource Names column. The Resource Names column is the last column of the Entry table. You can also use other methods for assigning resources, such as using the Assign Resources button or using the split window, which is the recommended approach to have the most control over how resources are assigned because Project 2010 makes several assumptions about resources assignments that might mess up your schedule or costs. Next, you will enter information for three people working on Project A+ and assign them to a few tasks using various methods.

To enter basic information about each person into the Resource Sheet and assign them to tasks using the Entry table and toolbar:

1.   *Display the Resource Sheet view.* Click the **View** tab, and then click the **Resource Sheet** button under the Resource Views group.

2.   *Enter resource information.* Enter the information from Figure A-37 into the Resource Sheet. The three resources names are **Kathy, Dan, and Scott**. The Std. Rate and Ovt. Rate for Kathy is **40**, and the Std. and Ovt. Rates for Dan and Scott are **30**. Type the information as shown and press the **Tab** key to move to the next field. When you type the standard and overtime rates, you can just type the number, such as 40, and Project 2010 will automatically enter $40.00/hr. The

standard and overtime rates entered are based on hourly rates. You can also enter annual salaries by typing the annual salary number followed by /y for "per year." Your screen should resemble Figure A-37 when you are finished entering the resource data.

Resource Name	Type	Material	Initials	Group	Max.	Std. Rate	Ovt. Rate	Cost/Use	Accrue At	Base Calendar
Kathy	Work		K		100%	$40.00/hr	$40.00/hr	$0.00	Prorated	Standard
Dan	Work		D		100%	$30.00/hr	$30.00/hr	$0.00	Prorated	Standard
Scott	Work		S		100%	$30.00/hr	$30.00/hr	$0.00	Prorated	Standard

Figure A-37. Resource sheet view with resource data entered

TIP: If you know that some people will be available for a project only part time, enter their percentage of availability in the Max Units column of the Resource Sheet. Project 2010 will then automatically assign those people based on their maximum units. For example, if someone can work only 50% of his or her time on a project throughout most of the project, enter 50% in the Max Units column for that person. When you enter that person as a resource for a task, his or her default number of hours will be 50% of a standard eight-hour workday, or four hours per day. You can also enter the number of hours each person is scheduled to work, as shown later.

3. *Assign resources to tasks*. Click the **View** tab, select the **Gantt Chart** button under the Task Views group, and then click the **Select All** button and switch back to the **Entry** table. Widen the Task Name column and move the split bar to reveal the Resource Names column, if needed.

4. *Assign Kathy to task 2, Identify stakeholders*. Click in the **Resource Names** cell for **row 2**. Click the list arrow, click on the **checkbox** by **Kathy**, and then press **Enter** or click on another cell. Notice that the resource choices are the names you just entered in the Resource Sheet. Also notice that after you select a resource by checking the appropriate checkbox, his or her name appears on the Gantt chart, as shown in Figure A-38. To assign more than one resource to a task using the list arrow, simply select another checkbox. Note that Project 2010 will assume that each resource is assigned full-time to tasks using this method since the task is in automatically schedule mode.

Task Mode	Task Name	Duration	Start	Finish	Predecessors	Resource Names	Jan 24, '10 T F S	Feb 28, '10 S M T	Apr 4, '10 W
	⊟ Project A+	64.5 days	Mon 2/1/10	Fri 4/30/10					
	⊟ 1 Initiating	10.5 days	Mon 2/1/10	Mon 2/15/10					
	1.1 Identify stakeholders	1 wk	Mon 2/1/10	Fri 2/5/10		Kathy	Kathy		
	1.2 Stakeholder register completed	0 days	Fri 2/5/10	Fri 2/5/10	2	☐ Dan	◆ 2/5		
	1.3 Stakeholder management strategy completed	0 days	Fri 2/5/10	Fri 2/5/10	2	☑ Kathy	◆ 2/5		
	1.4 Prepare project charter	1 wk	Wed 2/3/10	Wed 2/10/10	2FS-50%	☐ Scott			

Figure A-38. Resource assigned using the entry table

5. *Assign two resources to a task*. Click in the **Resource Names** cell for **row 5**. Click the **list arrow**, then click on the **checkbox by Dan and Kathy,** and then press **Enter**. Notice that both resource names appear in the Resource Names

column and on the Gantt chart for this task, and the task duration remains at 1 week.

6.   *Change the resource assignments.* Click in the **Resource Names** cell for **Task 2**, Identify stakeholders, click the **list arrow**, and add **Dan** as another resource. Notice that when you change an original resource assignment, Project prompts you for how you want to handle the change, as shown in Figure A-39. Click the **Exclamation point** symbol to read your options. *This is an important change!* In past versions of Project, resource additions would change schedules automatically unless the user entered them a certain way. Now you have much more control of what happens to your schedule and costs. In this case, we do want to accept the default of keeping the duration constant.

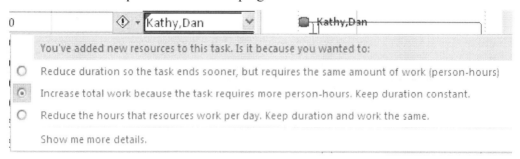

Figure A-39. Options when additional resources are added to tasks

7.   *Review the cost table.* Right-click the **Select All** button to the left of the Task Mode column heading and select **Cost**. Notice that costs have been added to the tasks where you added resources. Project assumes that people are assigned full-time to tasks. It is showing a cost of $2,800 each for Task 2 and Task 5. In the next section, you will see how to control resources entries even more.

To control resource and work assignments using the Resource details window:

1. Open the Resource Form. Click the **Resources** tab, and then click on the **Details** button under the Properties group. The Cost Table and Gantt Chart view is displayed at the top of the screen and a Resource Form is displayed at the bottom of the screen, as shown in Figure A-40. Also notice the symbol in the Indicators column showing that resources are overallocated. This is because Project 2010 assumes every task is assigned full-time, so since Kathy is scheduled on two tasks on the same day, it says she is overallocated.

> **TIP:** You can right-click on the lower screen to review see additional forms/views. You can click the Select All button at the top right of the screen to view different tables at the top of the screen. You want to make sure that resource and work hour assignments do not adjust your schedules in ways you did not intend.

2. Make tasks 2 and 5 manually scheduled. Click the **Select All** button and switch to the **Entry table**. Click the drop-down in the **Task Mode** column for Tasks 2 and 5 to make them **manually scheduled**. Notice the symbol in the Indicator column. This symbol means that tasks are currently overallocated. This is because when you assigned resources, Project 2010 assumed they were working full-time or 40 hours per week on each task. Since these two tasks have days that overlap, there is an overallocation.

3. Change the number of Work hours. Select Task 2, **Identify stakeholders** in the top window, and then click the **Work** column in the Resource Form window for Kathy in the lower part of your screen. Type **10h**, press **Enter**, and then click the **OK** button, as shown in Figure A-40.

Overallocation indicator **Manually scheduled task** **Changing # work hours**

OK button

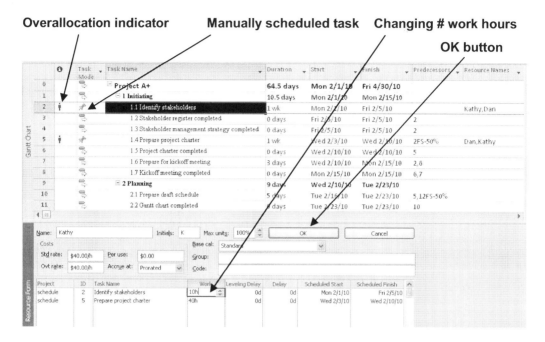

Figure A-40. Changing Work hours for tasks

4. *Enter the work hours and review the Gantt chart.* Click **Next** in the lower window, and change Dan's work hours to 10h for Task 2 as well. Notice in the Gantt chart that the duration for Task 2 is still one week, but there is still an overallocation. Click on **Task 5** in the upper window, and change the **Work** hours for both Dan and Kathy to 10h for this task as well. Note: Click the **Next** or **Previous** buttons in the lower window to access different resources, and click OK when finished. The overallocation indicator should now disappear because the number of hours has been reduced from the default of 8 hours per day, or 40 hours for a 5-day task

5. Examine the new cost information. Click the Select All button, and then click **Cost** to view the Cost table. Tasks 2 and 5 each show only $700 for Total Cost.

6. *Close the file without saving it.* Close the file, but do not save the changes you made.

Using the New Team Planner Feature

Another way to assign resources and reduce overallocations is by using the new Team Planner feature. Assume you have two people assigned to work on a project, Brian and Cindy, as shown in Figure A-41. Notice that Brian is assigned to work on both Task 1 and Task 2 full-time the first week. Therefore, Brian is overallocated. Cindy is scheduled to work on Task 3 full-time the second week, and Task 4, also scheduled for the second week, is not assigned yet.

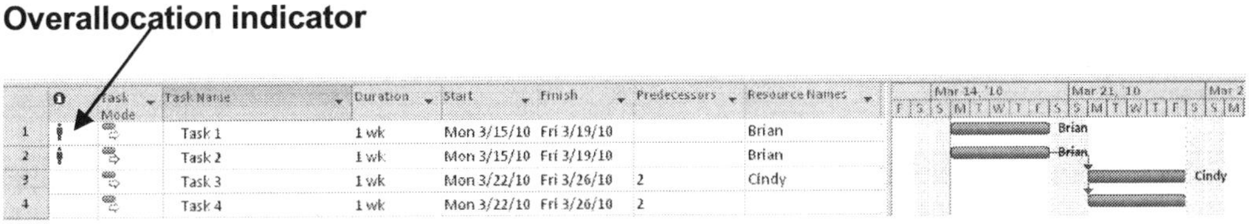

Overallocation indicator

Figure A-41. Overallocated resource

You can click on the Team Planner view under the View tab to see a screen similar to the top section of Figure A-42. Notice that Brian has both Tasks 1 and 2 assigned to him at the same time. These tasks and Brian's name display in red to show the overallocation. Cindy is assigned Task 3 the following week, and Task 4 is unassigned. By simply clicking and dragging Task 4 straight up so it is under Brian in Week 2 and Task 2 straight down so it is under Cindy in Week 1, you can reassign those tasks and remove Brian's overallocation, as shown in the bottom section of Figure A-42. Many people will appreciate the simplicity of this new feature!

Before moving tasks in the Team Planner View:

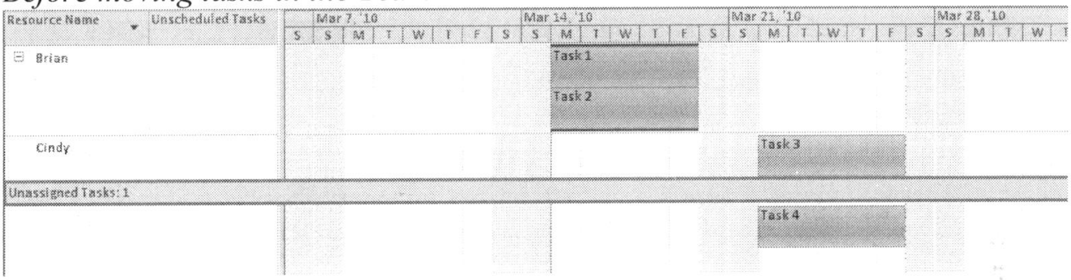

After moving tasks in the Team Planner View:

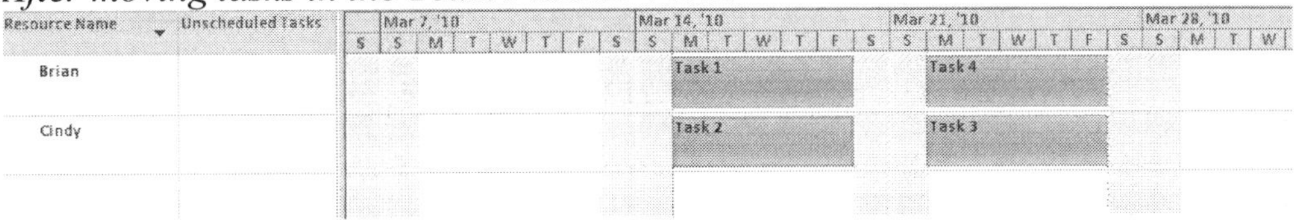

Figure A-42. Adjusting resource assignments using the Team Planner feature

Entering Baseline Plans, Actual Costs, and Actual Times

After entering tasks in a WBS, establishing task durations and dependencies, and assigning costs and resources, you are ready to establish a baseline plan. By comparing the information in your baseline plan to actual progress during the course of the project, you can identify and solve problems. After the project ends, you can use the baseline and actual information to plan similar, future projects more accurately. To use Project 2010 to help control projects and view earned value information, you must establish a baseline plan, enter actual costs, and enter actual durations. In the next series of steps you will use a new file called tracking.mpp that you downloaded from the companion Web site for this text (www.intropm.com).

To save a file as a baseline and enter actual information:

1. Open the file called tracking.mpp. Notice that this short project was planned to start on January 5, 2009 and end on February 13, have three resources assigned to it, and cost $11,200. Click the **Project** tab, click the **Set Baseline** button under the Schedule group, and click **Set Baseline**, as shown in Figure A-43.

Figure A-43. Saving a baseline

2. Save the file as a baseline. Examine the **Set Baseline** dialog box. Click the drop-down arrow to see that you can set up to ten baselines. Accept the default to save the entire project. Click **OK**. Notice that the Baseline column changes to blue.

3. Display the Tracking table. Click the **Task** tab, right-click the **Select All** button, and then click **Tracking** to view the tracking table. Move the split bar to the right to reveal all of the columns in the table. Move your mouse over each tracking button in the top line of the Schedule group to see what it does. Your screen should resemble Figure A-44.

Tracking table   Tracking buttons

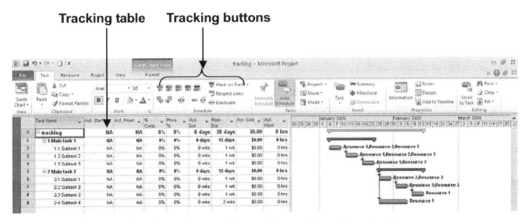

Figure A-44. Using the tracking table and tracking buttons

4. *Mark Tasks 2 though 4 as 100% complete.* Click the Task Name for Task 2, **Subtask 1 under Main task 1**, and drag down through Task 4 to highlight those tasks. Click the **100% Complete** button on the Ribbon. The columns with dates, durations, and cost information should now contain data instead of the default values, such as NA or 0. The % Comp. column should display 100%. Adjust column widths if needed. Your screen should resemble Figure A-45. Notice that the Gantt chart bars for those three tasks now have a black line through them.

Figure A-45. Tracking table information

5. *Enter actual completion dates for Task 6.* Click the Task Name for Task 6, **Subtask 1 under Main task 2**, click the **Mark on Track drop-down**, and then click **Update Tasks.** The Update Tasks dialog box opens. For Task 6, enter the Actual Start date as **1/26/09** (the same as the Current start date) and the Actual Finish date as **2/9/09** (later than the Current finish date), as shown in Figure A-46. Click **OK**. Notice how the information in the tracking sheet has changed.

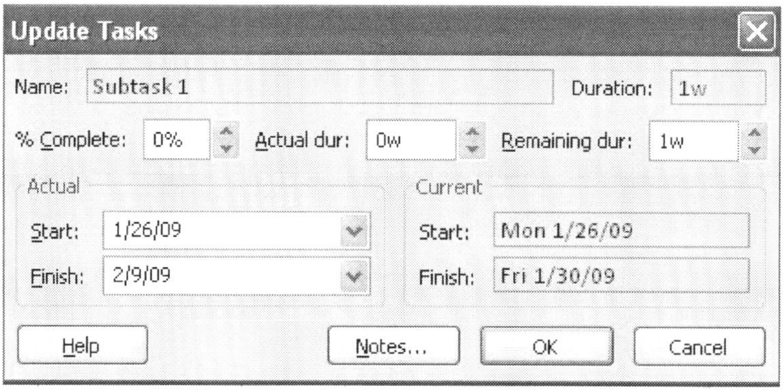

Figure A-46. Update Tasks dialog box

> 6. *View the Tracking Gantt chart*. Right-click on the far left of the screen where it says Gantt chart, and then click **Tracking Gantt** to quickly switch to that view. Move the **split bar** and adjust column widths as needed. Use the **horizontal scroll bar** in the Gantt chart window to the right (move the slider to the left) to see symbols on the Tracking Gantt chart. Use the Zoom slider on the lower right of the screen to adjust the timescale so you can see all of the symbols. Your screen should resemble Figure A-47. The blue bar for task 6 shows the actual time you just entered. Notice that the delay in this one task on the critical path has caused the planned completion date for the entire project to slip. Also notice the Indicator column to the far left. The check marks show that tasks are completed.

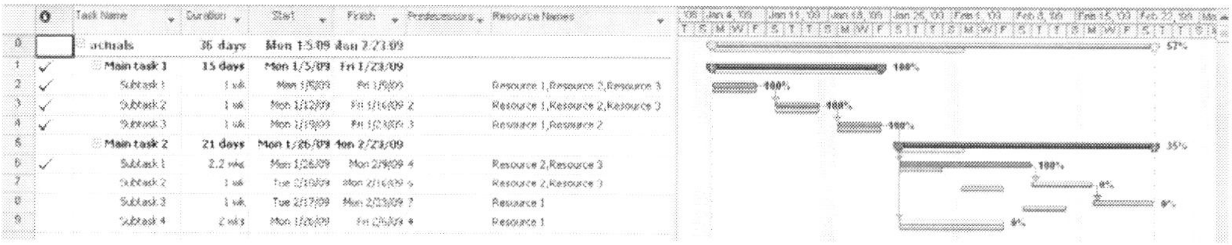

Figure A-47. Tracking Gantt chart view

> 7. *Save your file as a new file named actuals.mpp*. Click **File** on the Menu bar, and then click **Save As**. Name the file **actuals**, and then click **Save**.

Notice the additional information available on the Tracking Gantt chart. Completed tasks have 100% by their symbols on the Tracking Gantt chart. Tasks that have not started yet display 0%. Tasks in progress, such as Task 5, show the percentage of the work completed (35% in this example). The project summary task bar indicates that the entire project is 57% complete. Viewing the Tracking Gantt chart allows you to easily see your schedule progress against the baseline plan. After you have entered some actuals, you can review earned value information for the initiating tasks of this project.

VIEWING EARNED VALUE MANAGEMENT DATA

Earned value management is an important project management technique for measuring project performance. (See Chapter 7 of this text or other resources for detailed information on earned value management). Because you have entered actual information, you can now view earned value information in Project 2010. You can also view an earned value report using the new visual reports feature.

To view earned value information:

1. *View the Earned Value table.* Using the actual file you just saved (or downloaded from the companion Web site), click the **Select All** button, select **More Tables,** and double-click **Earned Value**. Move the split bar to the right to reveal all of the columns, as shown in Figure A-48. Note that the Earned Value table includes columns for each earned value acronym, such as SV, CV, etc., as explained in this text. Also note that the EAC (Estimate at Completion) is higher than the BAC (Budget at Completion) starting with Task 6, where the task took longer than planned to complete. Task 0 shows a VAC (Variance at Completion) of ($3,360.00), meaning the project is projected to cost $3,360 more than planned at completion. Remember that not all of the actual information has been entered yet. Also note that the date on your computer must be set later than the date of a completed task for the data to calculate properly.

	Task Name	Planned Value - PV (BCWS)	Earned Value - EV (BCWP)	AC (ACWP)	SV	CV	EAC	BAC	VAC
0	actuals	$11,200.00	$8,000.00	$10,400.00	($3,200.00)	($2,400.00)	$14,560.00	$11,200.00	($3,360.00)
1	Main task 1	$6,000.00	$6,000.00	$6,000.00	$0.00	$0.00	$6,000.00	$6,000.00	$0.00
2	Subtask 1	$2,400.00	$2,400.00	$2,400.00	$0.00	$0.00	$2,400.00	$2,400.00	$0.00
3	Subtask 2	$2,400.00	$2,400.00	$2,400.00	$0.00	$0.00	$2,400.00	$2,400.00	$0.00
4	Subtask 3	$1,200.00	$1,200.00	$1,200.00	$0.00	$0.00	$1,200.00	$1,200.00	$0.00
5	Main task 2	$5,200.00	$2,000.00	$4,400.00	($3,200.00)	($2,400.00)	$11,440.00	$5,200.00	($6,240.00)
6	Subtask 1	$2,000.00	$2,000.00	$4,400.00	$0.00	($2,400.00)	$4,400.00	$2,000.00	($2,400.00)
7	Subtask 2	$2,000.00	$0.00	$0.00	($2,000.00)	$0.00	$2,000.00	$2,000.00	$0.00
8	Subtask 3	$400.00	$0.00	$0.00	($400.00)	$0.00	$400.00	$400.00	$0.00
9	Subtask 4	$800.00	$0.00	$0.00	($800.00)	$0.00	$800.00	$800.00	$0.00

Figure A-48. Earned value table

2. *View the earned value chart.* Click the **Project** tab, and then click **Visual Reports** under the Reports group to open the Visual Reports dialog box. Click **Earned Value Over Time Report**, as shown in Figure A-49. Notice the sample of the selected report on the right side of the dialog box. If you have Excel and other necessary software, you could click View to see the resulting report as Project 2010automatically creates Excel data and a chart based on your current file. Click the **Close** button of the Visual Reports dialog box.

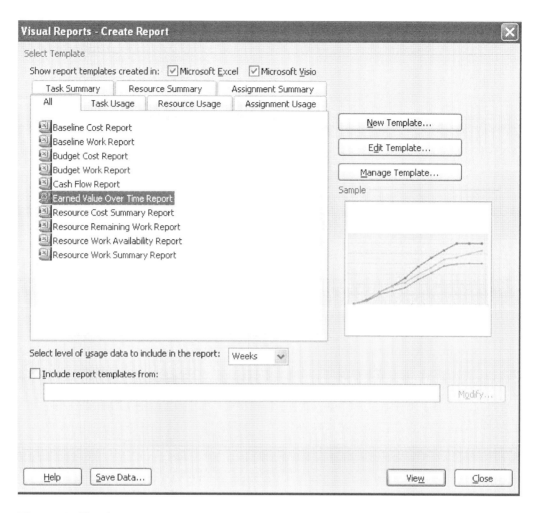

Figure A-49. Visual reports dialog box

3. *Save and close the file*. Click the **Save** button on the Standard toolbar, and then close the file. You can also exit Project 2010 and take a break, if desired.

Next you will use a few more features of Project 2010 to help tie your Project to your other applications.

INTEGRATING PROJECT 2010 WITH OTHER APPLICATIONS

Project 2010 provides many different tables, views, reports, and formatting features to aid in project communications, as you have seen in the previous sections. This section highlights some common reports and views. It also describes how to insert hyperlinks within Project 2010 to other project documents.

Common Reports

As you have seen, you can easily change and print out various table views in Project 2010, such as the Entry Table, Cost Table, Schedule Table, and so on. Many different reports are also available in Project 2010, categorized as follows when clicking the Reports button under the Project tab.

- Overview reports include:
  - Project Summary
  - Top-Level Tasks
  - Critical Tasks
  - Milestones
  - Working Days
- Current reports include:
  - Unstarted Tasks
  - Tasks Starting Soon
  - Tasks In Progress
  - Completed Tasks
  - Should Have Started Tasks
  - Slipping Tasks
- Costs reports include:
  - Cash Flow
  - Budget
  - Overbudget Tasks
  - Overbudget Resources
  - Earned Value
- Assignments reports include:
  - Who Does What
  - Who Does What When
  - To-do List
  - Overallocated Resources

- Workload reports include:

  - Task Usage

  - Resource Usage

- Custom allows you to customize and save your own report formats.

By selecting the Visual Reports button from the Project tab, you can access the following types of reports:

- Baseline Cost Report

- Baseline Work Report

- Budget Cost Report

- Budget Work Report

- Cash Flow Report

- Earned Value Over Time Report

- Resource Cost Summary Report

- Resource Remaining Work Report

- Resource Work Availability Report

- Resource Work Summary Report

Feel free to experiment with the various reports available in Project 2010 or to create your own.

Creating Hyperlinks to Other Files

Some people like to use their Project 2010 file as a main source of information for many different project documents. To do this, you can simply insert a hyperlink to other document files. For example, you can create a hyperlink to the file with the stakeholder register you listed as a milestone in your Task Name column earlier.

To insert a hyperlink within a Project 2010 file:

1. Open the **schedule.mpp** file. Use the file you saved earlier or download it from the companion Web site for this text. The Entry table and Gantt Chart view should display.

2. Select the task in which you want to insert a hyperlink. Click the Task Name for Task 3, **Stakeholder register completed**.

3. Open the Insert Hyperlink dialog box. Right-click, then click **Hyperlink**. The Insert Hyperlink dialog box opens, as shown in Figure A-50. You will have different folders visible based on your computer's directory structure.

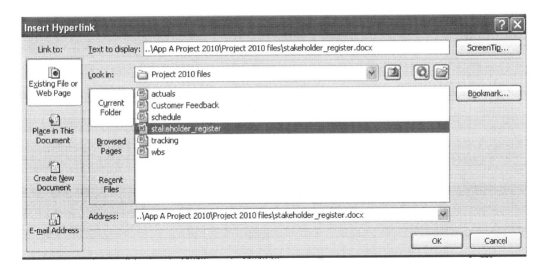

Figure A-50. Insert hyperlink dialog box

> 4. *Double-click the filename of the hyperlink file.* Change the **Look in:** information until you find where you have saved the files you downloaded for this appendix. Double-click the Word file named **stakeholder_register**, and then click **OK**. A Hyperlink button appears in the Indicators column to the left of the Task Name for Task 3. Move your mouse over the hyperlink button until the mouse pointer changes to the Hand symbol to reveal the name of the hyperlinked file. If you click on it, the file will open.

You have really just touched the surface of Project 2010's powerful features, but you probably know more than most people who have this software! There are several books with more detailed information on using Project 2010 that you can use to learn even more, or you can experiment with the software and Help feature to understand it more.

DISCUSSION QUESTIONS

1. What are some unique features of project management software?

2. What are the new features of Project 2010?

3. How do you create a WBS in Project 2010?

4. How do you enter task durations and establish dependencies between tasks?

5. What is the recommended method for assigning resources to tasks? Why is it the preferred method?

6. How can you use the Team Planner to assign resources and reduce overallocations?

7. How do you establish a baseline in Project 2010 and enter actual information?

8. What type of information do you see in the Earned Value table?

9. What are some of the reports built-in to Project 2010? Which ones do you think are commonly used?

10. How can you access other application files from within Project 2010?

EXERCISES

1. To make sure you understand the information in this appendix, perform the steps yourself. Print out the following screens or send them to your instructor, as directed:

   a. The adjusted Customer Feedback.mpp file as shown in Figure A-7.
   b. The Schedule table view for the Customer Feedback file, similar to Figure A-11.
   c. The Customer Feedback file filtered to show only critical tasks, similar to Figure A-15.
   d. The wbs file, similar to Figure A-21, but without the Closing tasks indented. Also type your first and last name after the word Initiating, the first Task Name.
   e. Create a new Project file called mywbs that shows the WBS for a generic project. Make the main categories phase 1, phase 2, phase 3, and phase 4. Include at least four tasks and one milestone under each of these main categories, using meaningful, fictitious names for them. Enter 0 for the duration of the milestones, but do not enter any durations for the other tasks. Be sure to indent tasks and show the outline numbers before printing.

2. Continue performing the steps in this appendix, starting with the section called Developing the Schedule. Print out the following screens or send them to your instructor, as directed:

    a. The schedule file with durations and dependencies entered, similar to Figure A-27. Type your first and last name after the word Initiating, the first Task Name, before printing or handing in the file.

    b. The earned value table, similar to Figure A-48. Again type your name after the word Initiating, the first Task Name.

    c. Continue performing the steps, even if you do not have to print out more screens. Write a one-to-two page paper describing the capabilities of Project 2010 and your opinion of this software. What do you like and dislike about it?

3. Use some of the information in the body of this text to practice your Project 2010 skills.

    a. Review the sample WBS for the Just-In-Time Training project provided in Chapter 4, Figure 4-10. Enter the WBS into Project 2010. Indent tasks and use the automatic numbering feature. Print or hand in your file.

    b. Use the information in Figure 4-14 for Project X to create a Gantt chart, as shown in Figure 4-18. Also create the network diagram for Project X, as shown in Figure 4-16. Make sure both will print out on one page each, then print or send them to your instructor Assume the start date was 6/9/09, or June 9, 2009.

    c. Make up actual information for Project X. Assume some tasks are completed as planned, some take more time, and some take less time. View and then print out or hand in the tracking Gantt chart.

4. If you are doing a team project as part of your class or for a project at work, use Project 2010 to create a detailed file describing the work you plan to do for the project.

    a. Create a detailed WBS, including several milestones, estimate task durations, link tasks, add tasks to the timeline, enter resources and costs, assign resources, and so on. Save your file as a baseline and print it out send it to your instructor, as desired.

b. Track your progress on your team project by entering actual cost and schedule information. Create a new baseline file if there have been a lot of changes. View earned value information when you are halfway through the project or course. Continue tracking your progress until the project or course is finished. Print or send your Gantt chart, Project Summary report, Earned Value table, and relevant information to your instructor.

c. Write a two- to three-page report describing your experience. What did you learn about Project 2010 from this exercise? How do you think Project 2010 helps in managing a project? You may also want to interview people who use Project 2010 for their experiences and suggestions.

COMPANION WEB SITE

Visit the free companion Web site for this text at **www.intropm.com** to access template files, online quizzes, Jeopardy-like games, Microsoft Project files, links to sites mentioned in the text, and other information to help you learn more about this important field. Instructors must contact the author at schwalbe@augsburg.edu to gain access to the instructor site. Anyone can access the student site.

END NOTES

[1]TopTenREVIEWS™, "Project Management Software," (http://project-management-software-review.toptenreviews.com) (accessed June 17, 2009).

Made in the USA
Lexington, KY
20 February 2013